Camping Tips & Ideas

The Ultimate 101 Camping Guide for Beginners

Table of Contents

Introduction 6

Chapter 1: Gear for Body Protection 7

    Clothing and Shoes.. 7

    First Aid 8

    Body Protection Tips and Tricks 8

Chapter 2: Camping Quarters 13

    Selecting a Campsite 13

    Selecting a Tent 15

    Other DIY Hacks and How to Tips 16

        Ambient Lighting 16

        Foam Floor Tiles 17

        Sleeping Bags 17

        Warm your Sleeping Bag 17

        Make Zippers User Friendly 18

        Floating Keys 18

Chapter 3: Food and Water Tips and Tricks 19

    Kitchen Camping Gear Needs 19

    Water Tricks and Tips 28

- Good Old Boiling Technique..................................28
- Filtration Systems...28
- Ultraviolet Filters...29
- Chlorine Based Treatment Solution 29
- Gravity Flow Filters 30
- How to Choose Water..30
- Prevent Contamination 30
- Food Tips, Tricks and Some Recipes......................31
  - Free Camping Recipes.......................................33
- Conclusion..39

Introduction

When going camping, there's a thin line between going overboard with your belongings and underdoing things. The problem with having so much camping gear is that it bogs you down, but it definitely helps make life convenient in a camp. While having less camping gear would mean mobility, but it can make you frustrated when it comes to convenience.

So, what do you need exactly when going camping? When it comes to camping, you generally should think about and prepare for 3 important areas, namely: your food and water, your shelter and sleeping area and lastly body maintenance items.

Once you understand what these three entails, camping will be a great experience with little to no mishaps experienced. So, read on and learn a lot of DIY tips and tricks

Chapter 1: Gear for Body Protection

When it comes to body maintenance, this simply means gear for maintaining your body—specifically, clothing, shoes, and first aid.

Clothing and Shoes

Clothing is an important item when going camping because this will help you be protected from the harsh environment. Depending on the season that you are camping and even elevation plays an important role. So, know well the environmental conditions of your camping spot so you would know what to pack.

Further, outdoor temperatures can change drastically. In summer times, weather can be hot during the daytime and can drop drastically low at night. So, be sure that you have the right clothing to protect you from the sun's harmful rays and the cold temperatures at night.

Another thing that you should look out for is activities that you want to enjoy during camping. You might go for a hike, swim, kayaking, boating, and others. So make sure that you have the right footwear too, not just the right clothing.

First Aid

The great outdoors also come with natural hindrances like bee stings, ticks that could carry Lyme disease, disease carrying mosquitoes and even poisonous plants. So, you should also be equipped to protect your body against these harmful elements. Aside from your clothes which are your first layer of protection, you should also have a first aid kit that can help relieve these nasties. But, the best line of defense is also prevention—some tips and tricks on how to prevent these nasties from happening will be provided below.

Body Protection Tips and Tricks

1) **Use Microfiber Towels** – these towels are small but very absorbent so it doesn't take up so much space but is very helpful especially when camping near bodies of water.

2) **Emergency Toilet** – if camping in spots with no basic amenities, then make your own emergency toilet with a milk crate, a bucket and a plastic. Place the milk crate upside down and make a hole in the middle just the size of the bucket's hole. The crate will serve as the

toilet seat and the bucket as the catcher. To use, place a plastic large enough to go into the bucket. Once done using, remove plastic, dispose of properly and add a new plastic for the next user.

3) **Keep Mosquitoes Away** – you can keep mosquitoes at bay by adding bundles of sage into your campfire. The smell of burning sage is a mosquito deterrent.

4) **Mini First Aid Kit** – when camping, you will be busy with so many activities that at times you will find yourself away from camp most of the time. So, it is only prudent to have a mini first aid kit that you can bring anywhere with you. By using an old Altoids tin or an old prescription bottle, fill it with band aids, alcohol prep pad, and ointments.

5) **Hand Wash Station** – as part of your body protection, hand washing is an important way to protect yourself from illness. Being at camp doesn't mean you have to forgo washing your hands because of difficulty getting water. This is easily remedied by making use of an empty laundry detergent dispenser.

6) **Make Single-use Soap** – with a peeler, peel a bar of soap. Each peel of soap becomes single use soap. Perfect for hand washing use and even for washing mosquito bites to relieve the itchiness.

7) **Single-use Ointment Packets** – bringing those whole tubes of ointment can be bulky. What to do? Cut up a straw into 1 to 1.5 inch lengths. Seal one end and fill with ointment, then seal the other end. Voila, you now have a single use ointment packs. You can even color code them for easy identification. Add to your mini first aid kit and you are good to go hiking and camping.

8) **Protect Your Tissue** – when in the wild, the weather can be temperamental and a quick rain can easily drench your paper towels. So, how to protect them? Easy, just repurpose a plastic coffee can—the Folgers plastic container is perfect for this. Just, make a vertical slit on the side of the can, where the piece of tissue comes out for easy access. You can also add a piece of tie in there for easy hanging of your waterproof tissue dispenser.

9) **Tick Deterrent** – as we have mentioned above, the great outdoors can be host to many disease carrying insects. So protect yourself against Lyme disease carrying ticks with this easy to make spray. Just mix 2 parts water and 1 part tea tree oil in a spray bottle. Spray these on pant cuffs, socks, shoes, and entrance to your tent. Repeat this process daily just before wearing your gear and going out on your daily activities.

10) **Get to Know Poisonous Plants** – as I have mentioned before, there are poisonous plants in the wild and by just brushing your skin against these leaves; it can cause an allergic reaction. Further, to eliminate any worrying, get to know the poisonous plants in the area, as some of these may not be around your geographical location—so there is no actual need to worry. One of the best ways to protect yourself is through prevention by getting to know these poisonous plants.

11) **Water Repellant Clothing** – when going camping, the type of clothing best used and packed are water repellant because even

though it repels water, the material is still breathable which allows air circulation.

12) **Layer Your Clothes** – when camping the best way to be ready for any temperature change is to layer on clothing. You can just remove layers of clothes if it is too warm or pile on clothes to keep you warm during inclement weather.

13) **Sunblock** – when you are outdoors, do not forget to protect your skin with sunblock. Likewise have protection for your eyes with an appropriate sunglass and an appropriate lip balm for your lips.

14) **Waterproof your Shoes** – if you are wearing canvas shoes during camping, you can easily waterproof them by covering it with beeswax. Do this by rubbing beeswax all over your shoes. Once it is sufficiently covered with beeswax, blows dry your shoes. This will melt the beeswax and create a transparent shield all around your shoes.

Chapter 2: Camping Quarters

Camping quarters essentially mean you bed and your tent. Now when going camping, it doesn't mean you have to forgo sleeping comfortably. In fact, the only way you can enjoy camping is when you are comfortable and can sleep well; otherwise you may dread the thought of camping in years to come.

Aside from your tent and mat, under the camping quarters would be your chairs—though chairs may not be necessary in some camping sites but it can come in handy. So, it is up to you if you want to have one or not.

Lights are also necessary in your camping quarters. Having a campfire is great but the light it gives won't be useful inside your tent. You don't want to be groping all the time inside your sleeping quarters. And most of all, you want to see inside your tent.

Selecting a Campsite

Most people don't think this through. Sometimes they choose a camp spot that's near the water or the first empty spot they get into. But, here are a lot of things to think through before choosing a spot:

- **Dead Trees** – steer clear of dead trees because this would mean falling branches. It can easily ruin your good tent. A good indicator of a dead tree is debris and downed limbs around the site.

- **Wind direction** – always choose a spot that's upwind or else you would be gulping smoke from your neighbor's campfire all day or night long.

- **Loud neighbors** – if you are a walk in, meaning you're not the first one to arrive in camp, choose a camp that's located away from loud neighbors for a good night's sleep. Or if you are one of those loud campers, then choose a spot among loud neighbors too...

- **Slope** – a slight slope may seem harmless while viewing your campsite, but waking up at a godforsaken hour to see the whole family slid to your side of the tent is not something to be happy about.

- **Rocks** – before setting up tent, make sure that you remove rocks and pebbles on the spot you are putting up tent. Little rocks may seem harmless as you put up your tent, but once you are lying down, these tiny rocks can feel like boulders poking you everywhere.

Selecting a Tent

If you are planning to buy a tent, the information below will help you choose one.

- **Frequency of Use** – if you will be using your tent frequently, then buy the best quality that money can buy. If you are rarely going to use it, then go for the cheap ones. For medium quality tents, buy one if you are planning to use it every now and then.

- **Size of Tent** – small tents are quite flexible when it comes to choosing a camping spot because of its small size. Bigger tents tend to be choosy and picky when it comes to camping spots because the spot should be large enough to accommodate it. So, when choosing the right size tent for you, think of how many people are going to use it.

Getting a very big tent for your convenience would also mean that more effort is needed to put it up and knocking it down. You can also go for two tents for your family—one for you and your partner and another one for the kids.

- **Tent Buying** – the key factor in selecting a tent is to check the poles, zippers and seams. The poles must be sturdy and should not be prone to easy breakage. Seams should be tightly woven or else insects and moisture can seep in here. Zippers should close and open seamlessly for ease of use. If all of these things are built sturdily, then chances are that tent is built to last a long while.

Other DIY Hacks and How to Tips

Ambient Lighting

You can easily augment light coming from your head lamp by strapping it on to a jug filled with water. The light from your small head lamp will be magnified several times by the jug of water.

Foam Floor Tiles

What's great about foam floor tiles is that it can double up as your mat or as flooring to your tent. It weighs less and easily covers up the hard ground and any protruding rock.

Sleeping Bags

While you and your partner may want to sleep in one sleeping bag, the trick here is to buy two single sized sleeping bags with full zippers. You can zip together these two bags to form a double sleeping bag for a cheaper price.

Warm your Sleeping Bag

Just before hitting the sack, you can warm your sleeping bag by slipping in a bottle filled with hot water. Let it warm your bed for at least 5 minutes before getting in. You can even use the bottle of hot water to warm your feet or other areas of your body that needs warming.

Make Zippers User Friendly

Zippers can be quite small especially if you are wearing gloves or mittens. Make them easier to handle by adding key rings which are easier to handle and faster to find. This can also hold true for clothing with zippers.

Floating Keys

If you are going kayaking or boating and have to bring some keys with you, then make sure that your keys can float. Do this by attaching a cork to your key. Do ensure that the cork you attach is enough to make it float. Say goodbye to sinking keys forever.

Chapter 3: Food and Water Tips and Tricks

Food and water are some of the arduous work when camping. Water especially, is a very important commodity, not unless you want to carry gallons and gallons of water around. There are ways to purify water from streams, lakes or rivers near your camp ground.

What about food? Commonly when camping, campers chow on canned foods. But there are lots of ways to enjoy good food even while camping. So, if you want to enjoy camp food staple, then you would need several camping gear to do this.

Kitchen Camping Gear Needs

1) **Ice Chest** – ice chest is great camping equipment because you can use this to keep your drinks cool and even bring some meat with you and keep them for days before cooking.

   - **Keep your Water Frozen** – instead of filling your ice chest with buckets of ice that only takes up space without really posing any other use other than keeping the ice chest cold, why not freeze your water. This frozen water becomes the cooling source and once melted, becomes a good source of cold drinking water.

- **Keep your meat in Zip Lock Bags** – place your frozen meat in zip lock bags. The rule of thumb is 1 zip lock bag is equal to one meal or one cooking. This will keep your melted meat juices inside the bag and not messing your other food and drinks inside the ice chest.

2) **Cooking Gear** – depending on what fits your need best, you can cook over a camp fire or camp grill or even bring your own camping stove. Either way, you have to be prepared for cooking because no camping trip is possible without eating. So let me show you the benefits and drawbacks of each cooking gear:

- **Camp Fire** – a camp fire provides both warmth and a source to cook from—it's like killing two birds with one stone. But be careful because the fires can be very hot and can easily overcook a meal, thus you should have the right cooking skillets for this. Also consider the amount of firewood you would need to bring for your entire stay. But, you also have the option of foraging for your firewood in the area.

- **Camp Grill** – well, who doesn't love barbecues? BBQs are an all-time favorite and a staple of many camping nights. Many camp spots have built in grills, but you can also bring your own griller. Aside from that, you would also need to bring your own charcoal that would last you for your entire camping trip.

- **Camping Stove** – by far, having a camping stove is the most convenient way to cook during camping. However, the cost of buying a camping stove can be a drawback, but if you are planning to go on camping regularly, then banking on one is a good idea.

3) **Cooking Utensils** – aside from the cooking equipment, you would also need cooking utensils. So, here is a quick list of the most important items you must have in this list.

- **Cast Iron Frying Pan** – I highly recommend a cast iron frying pan for camping because it is very versatile and can withstand high fires coming from a camp fire. You can use it to fry an egg, bacon, fish or even steak. You can also use it to cook cornbread muffin and even bake bread or cinnamon over a campfire. You can also cook stews in it and even meat dishes with sauces. Nonstick and light weight pans can release toxic chemicals when used over campfires. The only bad side to using cast iron frying pan is that it weighs a lot.

- **Tin Foil** – you can also cook food inside a tin foil and you can never go wrong. It protects your food from the elements like stray ash. Plus, you keep your food juices inside the tin foil. You can cook it over a camp grill or camp fire—very versatile.

- **Long Handled Cooking Spoon and Fork** – you can actually use short ones if using a camping stove. But for those who plan to cook over a camp grill and camp fire, then these tools will definitely come in handy.

- **Protective and Fire Resistant Gloves** – have this one especially if you are cooking using cast iron skillets because the handles can get really hot.

- **Multi-tools** – instead of bringing knife, kitchen shears, can opener, bottle opener and etc. separately, I suggest that you invest in a multi-tool to save on space.

4) **Fire** – no camping is complete without fire. Whether you are making fire to cook food or simply to bring warmth, fire is a focal point in camping. With fire comes several safety precautions that you need to look into.

- **Burn Rate** – as we have mentioned earlier, know how long your firewood lasts and from there buy or forage for as much as you need or ration out your use of firewood. Dry and lighter wood essentially burns faster. Usually, 12 to 14 split sections of log are enough to last you until midnight, including cooking your dinner. This is also true for your charcoal—brings more than what you think you need because you never know when emergencies may arise.

- **DIY Fire Pit** – you can easily make a DIY fire pit by stacking and encircling your fire with rocks. This is especially important if you have kids around, because it becomes a kind of barrier between them and direct fire. It also adds aesthetics to your fire pit.

- **Poker** – do have a good and sturdy poker in hand to adjust the fire all night long. You can make use of your long-handled fork for this or just find a sturdy branch. If little ones are with you, have a rule that only one man can use the poker—and that's you, for their safety.

5) **Starting a Fire** – watching people start a fire looks so easy and effortless, but try and make one yourself and you'll be cursing in no time. So, here are some handy tips and tricks for starting a fire to help you with the daily hurdle of starting a fire. Fire starters are highly recommended because they help in lighting up a fire or else, you are bound to use up more matchsticks than you could afford.

- **Toilet Paper Core** – if you fill toilet paper cores with lint from your dryer, these are great fire starters. But, you do have to prepare this long before your camping trip.

- **1 Dozen Fire Starter** – in an egg carton, place and fill each egg hole with lint. Cover lint with wax. To use, just cut off one egg hole and use as a fire starter.

- **Cotton Pads Dipped in Wax** – In melted wax, one by one dip circular cotton pads and allow to cool and harden. Makes as many and as much as you think you would use and store in a zip lock bag. To use, just add cotton pads on to logs and ignite.

- **Match Protection** – protect your matches by placing them in a plastic container. Then on the underside of the cover, glue sandpaper. You can also dip each matchstick in beeswax, allow to cool before dipping the other end and allow to cool before storage.

- **Buy from the Grocery** – if you are not fond of DIY, you can easily buy fires tarter sticks at the charcoal aisle in your favorite grocery store.

- **Kindling** – kindling are pieces of paper, dry twigs or anything that burns easily to start a fire. And if you need one, you can actually use Doritos chips as kindling.

6) **Fire Safety** – fire safety is a very important practice not just for adults but also for families with young kids on a camping trip. Being aware of fire safety rules will help prevent forest fires and any untoward accidents.

- **Flammable Clothing** – many synthetic garments are flammable especially when exposed to open flame. So please be aware of this and check the garments you are wearing or bringing to camp, especially those of your children.

- **Hot Fire Pits** - Firepits can get hot immediately, so please instruct your kids about this. That is why surrounding the pit with rocks is important because it creates a barrier between the fire and you and your kids.

- **Where To Build Fires** – as much as possible, build fires on existing campfire rings. Build your fire away from overhanging branches, leaves, dry grass, logs, rotten stumps and steep slopes. Keep your extra firewood away from your fire pit. Clear a ten foot diameter around your fire to prevent accidental spread of fire.

- **Don't Leave Fire Unattended** – never leave your fire unattended. And before throwing away your matchstick make sure that it is cold. Better yet, throw your matchstick into the fire.

- **Douse the Fire** – when you are done with your fire, douse it with water. With your poker move around the logs, sticks, embers and rocks to ensure that no burning embers are left. If water is scarce, use dirt to douse the fire and embers. But, do not bury your coals because this can smolder and cause fire.

Water Tricks and Tips

If you are hiking, camping and moving around in desolate areas, then chances are it is not possible to bring gallons of water with you. Therefore, you might need to rely from Mother Nature's vast reserves. But, is this water safe for drinking? Rather than rely on chances, why not bring with you a water purifying system. There are several ways to purify your water in the wild and here they are:

Good Old Boiling Technique

If you have the time and energy, boil water from the stream, lake, creek, spring or river for 30 minutes. This will kill a lot of known pathogens in your drinking water. Allow to cool before transferring sterilized water into water bottles.

Filtration Systems

There are many backpacking friendly water filtration systems that can be bought. Depending on your need, you can incest on small-sized filtration and purification systems. There are also larger sized filtration systems that you can leave in camp, while there are those that you can bring with you.

Ultraviolet Filters

Ultraviolet filters are easy to use but make use of batteries. This water sterilization method is made famous by SteriPen. When using this type of sterilization, 99.99% of virus, bacteria and protozoa are destroyed. However, sediments or chemicals are not removed by this process.

Chlorine Based Treatment Solution

Add a few drops of this solution to your water, shake and allow to sit for at least ten minutes and it can eliminate viruses and bacteria. However, not all protozoa will be eliminated plus it won't work against sediments and chemicals in the water. But, if you want to be very safe when it comes to your drinking water, you can the chlorine based solution after filtering your water. This ensures that it is really clean. To remove or mask the chlorine taste, you can add Gatorade or a citrus mix into the water.

Gravity Flow Filters

Gravity flow filters are quite tricky to use especially if you are using small water resources. It can be expensive too. But, no power source is needed to purify your water—just gravity which is free. This is typically the water filtration choice for many backpackers and camping enthusiasts because of its ease of use and it has no moving parts. Plus, it is the most practical of all filtration systems to boot.

How to Choose Water

Most of us would rather choose water that's running and flowing freely. But according to researchers, churning water have a lot of items and organisms suspended in it; compared to pooled water, where heavier particles have the chance to sink to the bottom.

Prevent Contamination

Between refills and use, your water container can harbor bad things. Therefore, it is important to air dry your container in between use. Even just a few drops of stale water left in your water bottle can be a host to growth of microorganisms. You can also sanitize your water container by rinsing it for several minutes with vinegar or baking soda.

Food Tips, Tricks and Some Recipes

When it comes to food, many are torn... Food lovers tend to load their backpacks or cars half filled with food. While some, go commando and only bring with them the barest of necessities. So, either way you don't have to give up delicious food just because you are out camping. You can still enjoy great food with these delicious hacks, tips, tricks and recipes.

1) **Brewed Coffee** – you don't have to settle for instant coffee while on a camping trip. Brewed coffee along with coffee grounds, you don't have to settle for these either... All you need is coffee filter and floss. Fill a coffee filter with the right amount of ground coffee beans and tie securely with dental floss. To use, place coffee beans and filter in a boiling cup of water and allow to steep for at least 5 minutes before drinking. Discard coffee beans and filter and enjoy a freshly brewed cup of coffee.

2) **Hanging Gear** – with the many cooking utensils and pans that you have in your primitive

camping kitchen it is more convenient is you have a hanging gear. You can easily make one with the help of a belt and S-hooks. Just strap the belt around a tree trunk, at least around chest level and add the S hooks. At the other end of the hook hang your camping kitchen gear for easy access.

3) **Prepping Meals** – for easy meal preparation, you can prepare meals at home. For example, if you are planning to cook steaks, you can marinate it and place them in zip lock bags ready to be cooked. If you want to grill some vegetables, you can cut the veggies, place inside zip lock bag and add the necessary spices. Then just grill or cook in a skillet by pouring all contents and cooking. Also, when you are making your camping menu keep in mind how long it takes to prepare a certain dish and just stick to the easy and less fussy ones. Also choose dishes that have common spices for fewer items to bring.

Free Camping Recipes

Campfire Crescent Rolls

This is a perfect way to start your day with freshly baked rolls. You can add your favorite jam or filling inside or go for pigs in a blanket.

Ingredients:
1 crescent rolls
Hotdogs
Nutella or jam

Directions:

1) Open the package of crescent rolls and cut it into 4-equal strips around 1 to 1.5-inch in length.
2) Unroll 1 strip of dough and weave around a clean y-branch. Slather the middle of the dough with your favorite jam or Nutella or piece of chocolate and continue braiding the dough. You can also use hotdogs and place them in the middle of the braided dough.
3) Place over fire and cook until dough is golden brown and cooked.

Campfire Corn and Mushroom Quesadilla

Ingredients:
1 cup shredded pepper jack cheese
4 flour tortillas
Pepper and salt to taste
½ cup corn
10 button mushrooms, thinly sliced
½ medium red onions, sliced thinly
2 tsps oil

Directions:

1) You can prepare and cut mushrooms ahead of time and store in a zip lock bag all by itself. Try to cook quesadillas within 1-2 days of slicing, or you can buy those precut mushrooms which will last longer up to 3-4 days.
2) Combine sliced onions, oil, corn, pepper and salt. Place in a foil packet and seal well. If planning to cook later, store in a zip lock bag.
3) To cook, remove foil packet from plastic bag, place on grill and cook for at least 8 minutes or until veggies are cooked.
4) Meanwhile, prepare flour tortilla and evenly divide cheese into the middle of the flour

tortilla. Divide into 4 the cooked veggies and add on each tortilla.
5) Fold tortilla in half, place in a foil packet and seal. Grill for at least 2-3 minutes per side before serving.

Three Cheese Potatoes in a Foil

Ingredients:
½ cup cheddar cheese
½ cup shredded part skim mozzarella cheese
½ cup crumbled cooked bacon
2 tbsps butter
¼ tsp pepper
½ tsp salt
1 tbsp minced chives
3 tbsps grated Parmesan cheese
1 medium onion, chopped
3 large potatoes, peeled and cut into ½-inch cubes

Directions:

1) In a large foil packet, place cubed potatoes, butter, pepper, salt, minced chives, Parmesan cheese, and chopped onions. Seal and place in a zip lock bag. Seal and place in ice chest.
2) In a small zip lock bag, combine cheddar cheese, mozzarella cheese and crumbled cooked bacon. Seal and place in ice chest.
3) Once ready to cook, remove potato foil packet from plastic bag and grill or cook on campfire for 15 minutes per side or until potatoes are tender.

4) Once potatoes are tender, open foil and sprinkle the cheese and bacon mixture. Cover and return to grill. Cook for another 3-5 minutes to melt cheese. Serve and enjoy.

No Mess Pancake Batter

Pancakes are great morning wake me ups, especially for kids and adults alike. This neat trick will help you make fuss free pancakes at camp.

Ingredients:
Pancake Mix
Empty Ketchup Bottle

Directions:

1) Make the pancake batter following package instructions while still at home. Once done, transfer batter into an empty and clean ketchup bottle.
2) Store pancake batter inside an ice chest.
3) To cook, grease a cast iron skillet and squeeze out enough pancake batter for one pancake. Cook as you would normally cook pancakes. Serve with butter, honey or your favorite jam or Nutella.

Conclusion

Armed with all these knowledge, camping will be so much fun. There may be a few minor glitches but if you stick to the tips and tricks I have laid out for you, I assure you that you won't run into major camping problems.

I also hope that you'll enjoy the easy and delicious camping recipes I have added for your convenience and enjoyment. These are truly delicious, easy and out of this world that even kids will love it.

All in all, I hope you'll have some clean and good fun while camping without breaking the bank!

Copyright © 2015. All rights reserved.

Except as permitted under the United States Copyright Act of 1976, reproduction or utilization of this work in any form or by any electronic, mechanical, or other means, now known or hereafter invented, including xerography, photocopying, and recording, and in any information storage and retrieval system, is forbidden without written permission.

The ideas, concepts, and opinions expressed in this book are intended to be used for educational and reference purposes only. Author and publisher claim no responsibility to any person or entity for any liability, loss, or damage caused or alleged to be caused directly or indirectly as a result of the use, application, or interpretation of the material in this book.

Printed in Great Britain
by Amazon.co.uk, Ltd.,
Marston Gate.